Will I live forever?

Carolyn Nystrom

Illustrated by Jo-Anne Shilliam

CANDLE
BOOKS

Do you ever think about dying?
I do. And my thoughts are quiet,
sad, scary thoughts.

Once a tiny bird flew straight at our window
and it hit the glass with a thud.

It fell to the ground, fluttered,
then lay still. I started to cry.
I ran outside and picked it up.
I wanted to help it fly again.
But the bird lay still in my hand.
I yelled for Mum.

Mum looked sad too.
"The bird is dead," she said.
"We have to bury it in the ground."

"No! No!" I yelled. "I want to keep
it in my room. Maybe it will live again."

"That won't happen,"
Mum said quietly.

Mum and I buried the bird in our garden.
A small feather clung to my finger.
I put it in my pocket.

Later, I sat holding the feather and thought long, scary questions about death.

Where is Heaven?

Why do birds and animals and people die?

Will I die some day?

Does it hurt to die?

How long does being dead last?

10

My mum came and sat beside me.
"It's all right to cry," she said.
Then we talked about
my questions.

Mum began by telling me
the story of God making
the world.

The world was beautiful then –
perfect – with trees, flowers,
even little birds.

God made a man and a woman
and He let them live in that
beautiful place.

"You may have everything here except one tree," God said. "If you eat fruit from that tree you will die."

At first the man and woman obeyed God, but they became more and more curious.

Maybe God did not really mean what He said, they thought.

So one day they ate fruit from the tree.

Genesis 1–3

Ever since that time, every man, woman, plant, or animal that lives eventually dies.

Romans 5:12–21; 8:18–23

But God does not want His people to be dead forever. So Jesus came to make up for the wrong the first man and woman had done.

Jesus lived. But He was different from any other man who lived. Jesus never disobeyed God.

Then Jesus died. But His death was different too.

JESUS CAME BACK TO LIFE!

Acts 2:22–24; 2 Corinthians 5:21

15

When an animal dies,
its body stops moving.
It can't see or hear or
feel anything anymore.
It can't breathe. Its heart
doesn't beat.

In a few days it will begin to soften
and smell bad. The body slowly
turns back into soil.

When a person dies, the same thing happens to his or her body. That's why we bury it in a cemetery.

We feel sad and sometimes we cry because we feel lonely without that person who died.

But a person is more than a body.

Inside is the "real me", the part that
thinks and feels and loves and makes
me different from any other person
in the world. It is called the soul.

As soon as one of God's people dies, the soul goes to heaven to be with Jesus.

And Jesus has made his or her place in heaven exactly what that person likes best.

Luke 16:19–31; Philippians 1:21–23

Later God will even make his or her
body new and take it to heaven also.
The new body will be perfect –
just like heaven.

It will not be broken or hurt or sick or ugly. Because Jesus came to earth and died and came back to life, we can live forever in heaven with Him. And forever never ends.

1 Corinthians 15; 1 Thessalonians 4:13–18

When Jesus was about to die He told His friends, "Don't be sad. I am going away to make heaven ready for you. But someday I'll come back and take you to heaven with Me."

John 14:1–19

The Bible says that heaven is too wonderful for our minds to understand. But it is fun to imagine.

Close your eyes and try.

Isaiah 65:17–25; 1 Corinthians 2:9

Think of the most beautiful thing you have ever seen.

Was it a mountain? A field full of wild flowers? A sunset? A basketful of puppies?

24

Or something totally different –
something no one but you
would think is beautiful.

Now open your eyes.

Heaven is even more beautiful
than that.

Revelation 21

Think again. When have you felt happiest in your whole life? On a trip to the zoo? On Christmas morning?

Catching raindrops on your tongue? Or sitting quietly and holding your favourite pet?

You will be happier than that in heaven.

Revelation 22

What do you like to do more than anything?

Play football? Lie on your back in tall grass and watch clouds?

What would you choose if you could do anything you wanted? Fly a plane? Build a city on Mars?

In heaven you will do things even more
wonderful – and you will enjoy them
even more.

Revelation 7:9–17

Think of someone you love.

Do you sometimes get angry and want them to leave you alone? Or do you worry that they don't like you as much as you like them?

Do you wish you could tell them something – only the words don't come out right?

In heaven you can know your friends perfectly. They will know you too. And you will love each other all the time.

1 Corinthians 13:8, 12; 1 John 3:2

31

In heaven you'll meet lots of other people too, people who lived a long time before you were born: your great-great-great-grandmother and King David and the apostle Paul. And all of you will know Jesus.

Jesus will take care of you in heaven.

"But Mum," I asked, "will the bird that died today be alive in heaven?"

"I don't know." Mum was quiet for a moment. "But Jesus is making heaven perfect for you. If you still want that bird when you go to heaven, I'm sure your bird will be there."

I sat for a while looking at my feather, but my thoughts weren't so sad and scary anymore.

I think I'll keep that feather in my bedroom.